Alphabet *of*
INSECTS

by Barbie Heit Schwaeber
Illustrated by Katy Bratun, Thomas Buchs, Allen Davis, John Paul Genzo,
Kristin Kest, Katie Lee, Larry Mikec and Daniel J. Stegos

SMITHSONIAN INSTITUTION

Book copyright © 2007 Trudy Corporation
and the Smithsonian Institution, Washington, DC 20560.

Published by Soundprints, an imprint of Trudy Corporation, Norwalk, Connecticut.
www.soundprints.com

Illustrations by Katy Bratun for the poster and the letter H
       Thomas Buchs for the cover, poster, title page, glossary and the letters A and L
       Allen Davis for the poster and the letters C and P
       John Paul Genzo for the poster and the letter G
       Kristin Kest for the cover, poster, title page and the letters B and S
       Katie Lee for the cover, poster, half title page, title page, glossary and the letters J and M
       Larry Mikec for the cover, poster and the letter F
       Daniel J. Stegos for the cover, poster, glossary and the letters D, E, I, K, N, O, Q, R, T, U, V, W, X, Y and Z

Book design: Marcin D. Pilchowski
Editor: Tracee Williams
Production editor: Brian E. Giblin

First Paperback Edition 2008
10 9 8 7 6 5 4 3 2 1
Printed in China

Acknowledgments:
    Our very special thanks to Gary Hevel of the Department of Entomology at the Smithsonian's National Museum
of Natural History for his curatorial review of this title.
    Soundprints would also like to thank Ellen Nanney and Katie Mann at the Smithsonian Institution's Office of Product
Development and Licensing for their help in the creation of this book.

ISBN 978-1-59249-992-2 (pbk.)

The Library of Congress Cataloging-in-Publication Data below applies only to the hardcover edition of this book.

Library of Congress Cataloging-in-Publication Data

Schwaeber, Barbie.

Alphabet of insects / by Barbie Heit Schwaeber ; illustrated by Katy Bratun ... [et al.].—1st ed.
   p.   cm.
ISBN 978-1-59249-725-6
1. Insects—Juvenile literature. 2. Alphabet books—Juvenile literature. I. Bratun, Katy, ill. II. Title.
QL467.2.S386 2007
595.7—dc22
                     2007029675

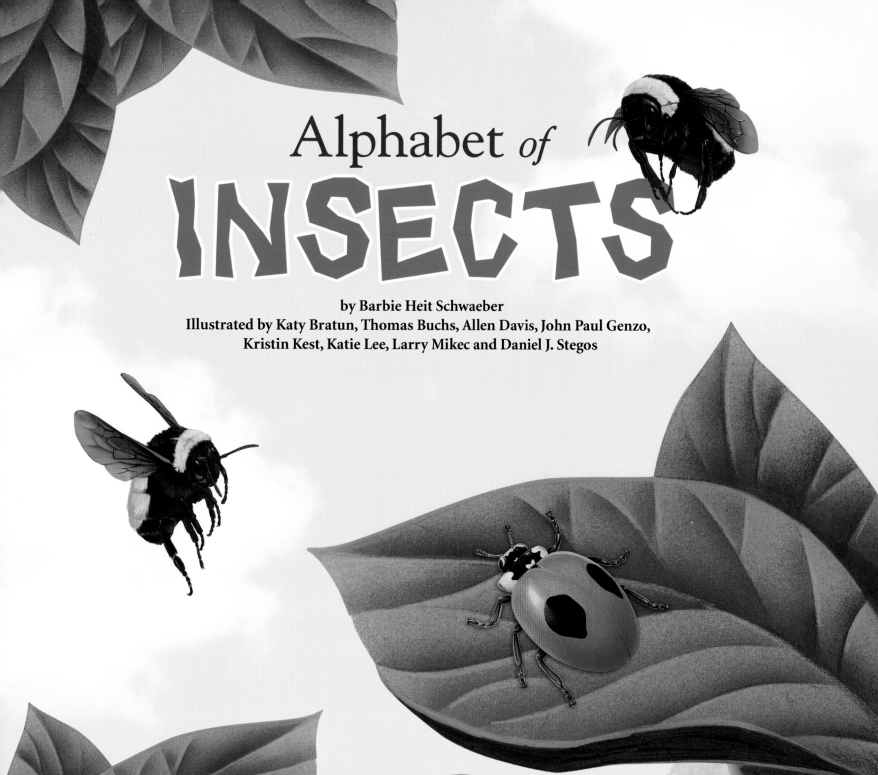

Alphabet *of* INSECTS

by Barbie Heit Schwaeber

Illustrated by Katy Bratun, Thomas Buchs, Allen Davis, John Paul Genzo,
Kristin Kest, Katie Lee, Larry Mikec and Daniel J. Stegos

Soundprints

A is for Aphid.

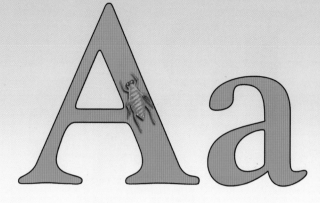

The aphid likes to eat green plants.
He thinks they are the best.
But to a farmer or a gardener
an aphid is a pest.

Bb

B is for **Bumblebee.**

A bumblebee as you can see
has yellow stripes and small black wings.
You may think this insect's cute
but don't get close—it stings!

C is for Cricket.

You might see a cricket.
He'll be jumping all around.
Listen very carefully
to hear his chirping sound.

Cc

Dd

D is for **Damselfly.**

The damselfly is colorful.
She has six long legs.
When it's time, she flies to water
then she lays her eggs.

E is for **Earwig**.

The earwig is quite active.
This insect can be found
in your house or garden
crawling all around.

Ee

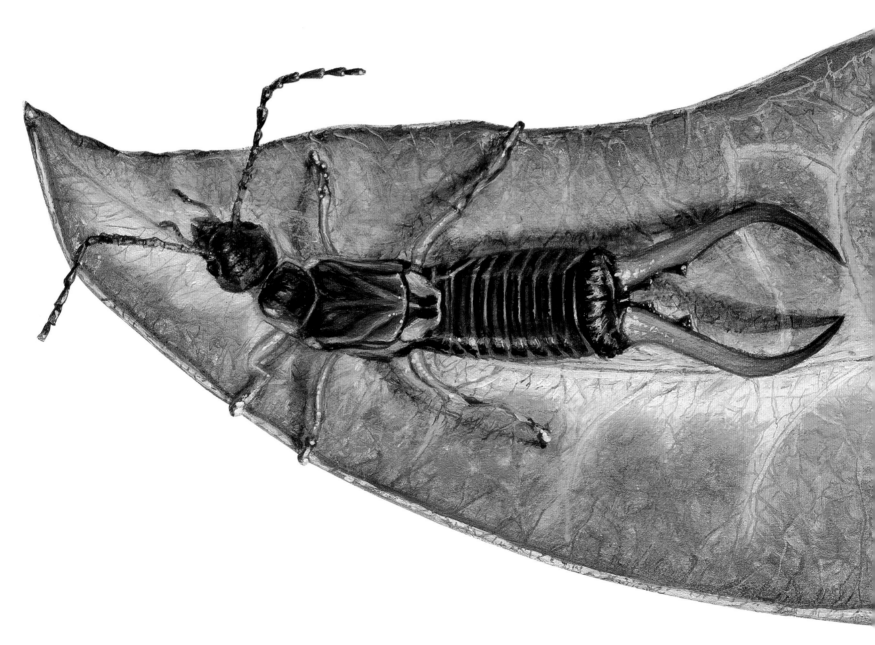

Ff

F is for **Firefly**.

Now let's look for a firefly!
It can be found at night.
You can spot this insect
when you see its flashing light.

Gg

G is for **Grasshopper**.

The grasshopper is hard to catch.
Would you like to know why?
She has two legs and uses them
to jump up very high.

Hh

H is for **Harlequin Cabbage Bug.**

This insect is a stinkbug.
And here's how you can tell:
If you get too close you'll know
it has an awful smell.

Ii

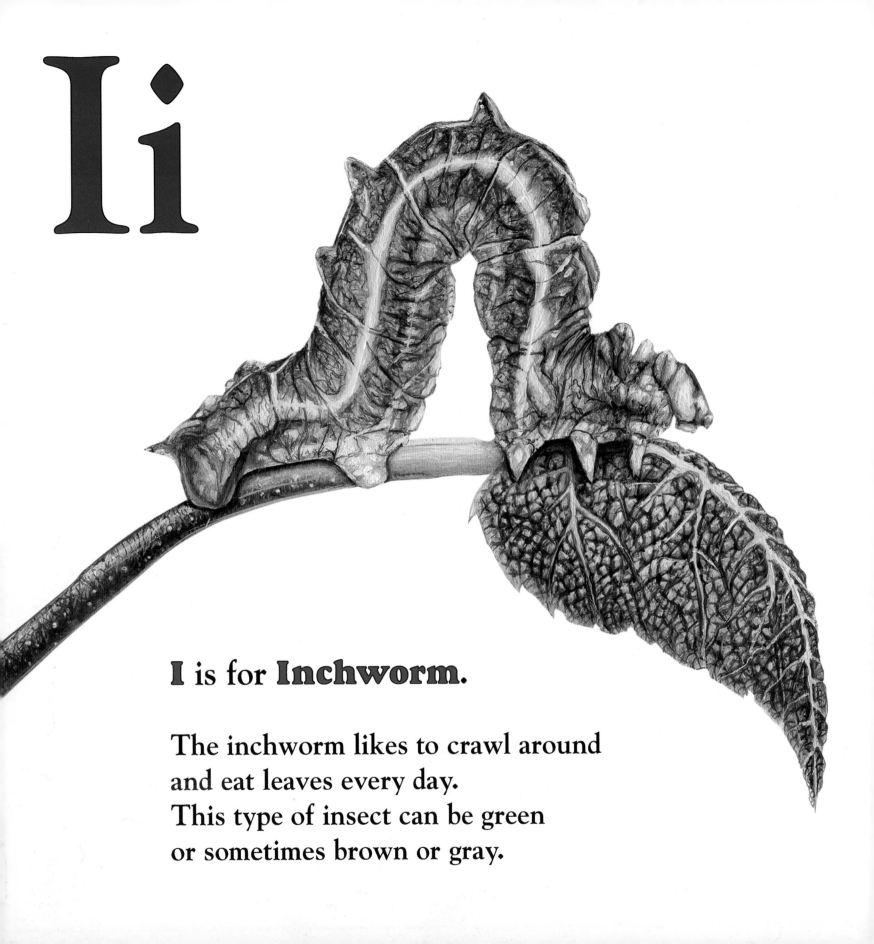

I is for **Inchworm**.

The inchworm likes to crawl around
and eat leaves every day.
This type of insect can be green
or sometimes brown or gray.

J is for **Japanese Beetle.**

If you look on this bug's head
you'll find a green spot there.
When he's scared he rolls on his back
with his feet up in the air.

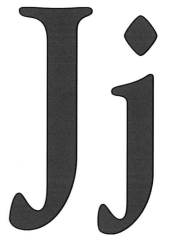

Kk

K is for **Katydid**.

This insect is shaped like a leaf
and she is colored green.
She hides in trees and blends right in
so she cannot be seen.

L is for **Ladybug**.

You might find this insect
in your yard or on your rug.
Some people think that it's good luck
to find a ladybug.

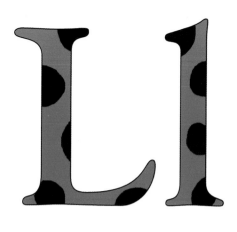

M is for **Monarch Butterfly**.

Monarch butterflies are beautiful.
They are orange, black and white.
If you see them in your garden,
it's such a lovely sight.

Mm

Nn

N is for **Nymph.**

This mayfly nymph will grow and change
and then as a result,
it will look quite different
by the time it's an adult.

O is for **Olive Fruit Fly.**

An olive fruit fly might be found
in salad, and here's why:
Olives are the favorite food
of this tiny fly.

Oo

Pp

P is for **Praying Mantis.**

A praying mantis hunts for
other insects night and day.
If you were an insect
you would try to stay away.

Q is for **Queen Leafcutting Ant.**

This tiny ant with her sharp mouth
cuts leaves she moves around.
She uses them to build her nest
deep under the ground.

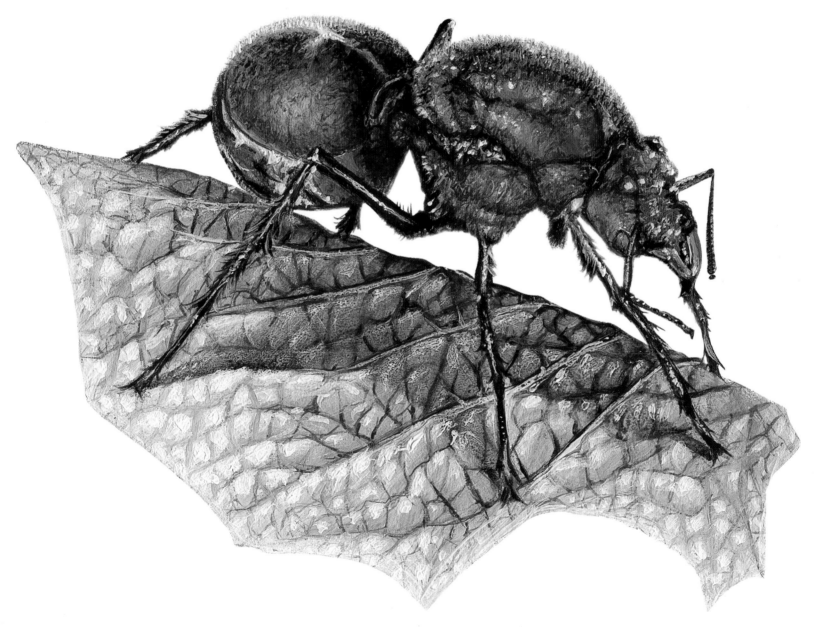

Rr

R is for **Redhead Ash Borer.**

This red insect likes to eat
any kind of wood.
A rotten log, a fresh cut tree,
he'd eat them if he could.

S is for **Sphinx Moth**.

Keep your eye out for the sphinx moth
because she flies with speed.
Look closely and you'll see her
on a flower, bush or weed.

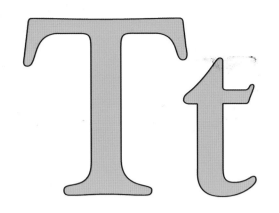

T is for Termite.

This insect causes trouble.
It eats houses just like yours.
This small white bug could eat the walls,
the window sills and floors.

U is for **Unicorn Caterpillar.**

These caterpillars lay their eggs
high in the trees they climb.
The tiny eggs are often hatched
three hundred at a time!

Uu

V is for **Velvet Ant.**

A velvet ant is covered
with soft and furry hair.
This insect is a type of wasp.
It could sting you, so beware!

Vv

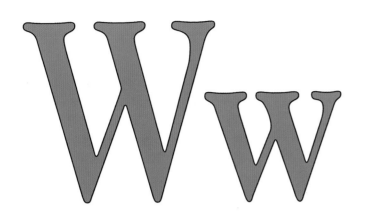

W is for **Weevil.**

When you spot this insect
there will surely be no doubt
that you have found a weevil,
just look at his long snout.

Xx

X is for **Xyelidae**.

This bug is a sawfly.
It's like a wasp but not the same.
It's rather small and has two wings
and Xyelidae is its name.

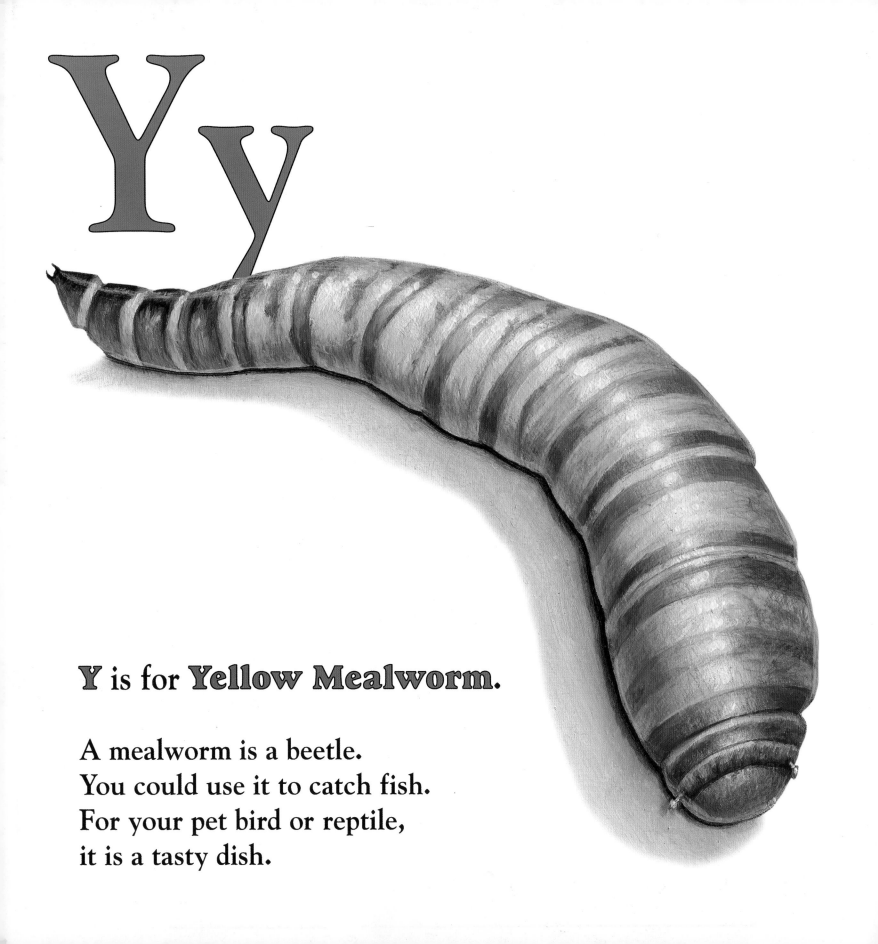

Yy

Y is for Yellow Mealworm.

A mealworm is a beetle.
You could use it to catch fish.
For your pet bird or reptile,
it is a tasty dish.

Z is for **Zebra Caterpillar.**

This caterpillar, you can see
has stripes both black and white.
What animal is it named for?
If you say zebra, you are right!

GLOSSARY

APHID: An aphid is a tiny insect that sucks juices from green plants. Aphids often spread viruses that can be harmful to the plants they eat. They are known for destroying fruit trees and vegetable crops. This is why farmers are not happy when they see aphids in their fields.

BUMBLEBEE: A bumblebee is a flying insect, usually recognized by its black body with yellow stripes. Its body is covered with a fiber called pile, making it look fuzzy. Two types of bumblebees can sting: the queen bee (female bee) and the worker bee (food-collecting bee.) Although this insect might look cute and fuzzy, don't even think about petting a bumblebee!

CRICKET: A cricket is famous for the chirping sound made only by the male cricket. The insect makes this sound by rubbing its wings together. There are two types of cricket songs: a calling song and a courting song. The calling song is used to attract females and keep other males away. The courting song is a quiet song played when a female is near. What may seem like an annoying sound to you is probably like music to the ears of a female cricket.

DAMSELFLY: A damselfly is a brightly-colored insect with a thin body and long wings that fold together when at rest. It looks similar to a dragonfly but it is much slower and weaker. People are sometimes frightened by the damselfly but there is no need to be—the damselfly is not able to sting. They do, however, fly very fast...so get out of their way!

EARWIG: An earwig is a nocturnal insect, meaning it is active at night. It has a long, flat body with a pair of large pincers in the back that can open and close. It is not usually harmful but it likes to be hidden. If the earwig does not feel safe or if it is threatened, this insect can bite. You don't want to be bitten by an earwig—its bite is very powerful.

FIREFLY: The firefly, also called a lightning bug, is a type of beetle that produces flashes of light to attract mates. Most fireflies are nocturnal, but there are some types that are active during the day. It can be a fun activity to capture fireflies in a jar and watch them glow—just remember to punch holes in the lid and let them go free when you're done.

GRASSHOPPER: The grasshopper is able to leap by using its long hind legs. Unlike some insects, grasshoppers have chewing mouth parts which they use to eat plants and vegetation. Farmers or gardeners might have a hard time capturing these jumpy bugs!

HARLEQUIN CABBAGE BUG: The harlequin cabbage bug belongs to a family of insects known as stinkbugs. These interesting little creatures have the ability to let out an awful smell to keep enemies away and protect themselves. They can often be found sitting on the plants they like to eat. If you happen to find a harlequin cabbage bug near a beautiful flower, you might think twice before bending down to smell the flower!

INCHWORM: An inchworm hides from its predators by camouflaging or blending itself into its surroundings. It can be green, gray or brown and is sometimes mistaken for a twig. It moves from back to front—its back side comes forward and then its front side follows giving the idea that it is measuring its progress.

JAPANESE BEETLE: A Japanese beetle is a copper-colored insect with a shiny green spot on top of its head and body. Whenever this insect is approached, it will stick its hind legs up in the air. These legs are spiny and they are the Japanese beetle's way of saying "keep away."

KATYDID: The katydid, a green insect related to the grasshopper and the cricket, produces a shrill sound by rubbing its wings together, just like its relatives. Some say it sounds like this: "Katy did, Katy didn't." This is how the insect got its name!

LADYBUG: A ladybug is a small, round, brightly-colored and spotted beetle. It eats aphids and other small insects, and sometimes plants. Ladybugs are harmless insects that are often thought of as being cute. Some people even consider it good luck to have a ladybug land on them and bad luck to harm one. The next time one lands on you, try making a wish.

MONARCH BUTTERFLY: The Monarch butterfly is one of the easiest types of butterflies to recognize with its wings shaded in a beautiful black and orange pattern. In fact, they are so beautiful that many people make butterfly gardens just to attract this type of butterfly. Monarchs are known for their long annual migrations in which they travel south from August through October, and come back north in the spring. During these migrations, the female lays her eggs for new Monarchs to be born.

NYMPH: A nymph is a very young insect, almost like a newborn baby would be to a human. The mayfly nymph lives in or near water. This nymph will go through metamorphosis, meaning its entire body will change completely before it becomes an adult. The mayfly nymph is also referred to as a Naiad, which in Ancient Greek mythology is actually a lovely woman.

OLIVE FRUIT FLY: An olive fruit fly is a type of insect that only eats one type of food—the olive plant. Some fruit flies work hard to keep harmful weeds and insects away from the plants they visit. This is not true for the olive fruit fly! This insect has the ability to ruin an entire olive crop by damaging the fruit. If you like olives in your salad, you would not want to eat near the olive fruit fly.

PRAYING MANTIS: The praying mantis can be found all over the world, although most live in tropical environments. It is usually brown or greenish in color and here is how it got its name: While this insect is at rest, it folds its legs in a position that makes it look like it is praying. If it really could pray, it would probably wish for other insects to come along. A praying mantis is a predatory insect, meaning it hunts other insects for its food.

QUEEN LEAFCUTTING ANT: The queen leafcutting ant is a female member of this species of ants. She has long wings and very sharp "teeth" in her mouth that make it possible for her to cut leaves and move them all around. After she lays her eggs in her nest, the queen leafcutting ant loses her wings. If you see a tree that is missing its leaves, chances are there is a leafcutting ant nest nearby.

REDHEAD ASH BORER: The redhead ash borer has a red head (as you've probably guessed) with fine yellow bands of hair on its body. It has long legs and antennae and it lives and breeds in dying or recently cut trees. The redhead ash borer will attack almost any type of wood, making it unusable for builders or even for use as firewood.

SPHINX MOTH: The sphinx moth is one of the fastest flying insects. It is able to fly at over 30 miles per hour! It feeds on nectar from flowers and can sometimes be seen hovering over plants and moving rapidly from side to side. This type of activity in sphinx moths is known as "swing hovering."

TERMITE: The termite, sometimes known as the white ant, is a destructive insect that causes damage to houses, buildings and forests. Although these insects resemble ants, they are not similar in any other way. They are generally softer, slower and fatter than ants and they are usually white in color with a darker colored head. All termites feed on wood and are very destructive so keep an eye out for them around your house!

UNICORN CATERPILLAR: The unicorn caterpillar is born on the bottom side of a leaf. It spends its day feeding on plants with groups of other caterpillars. During the winter months, the unicorn caterpillar buries itself deep under the soil. It is camouflaged on leaves by its skin color. If it is threatened, the unicorn caterpillar holds up its front and hind ends to attack its predator with a harmful acid. Steer clear of this caterpillar.

VELVET ANT: Believe it or not, a velvet ant is not an ant at all. It's actually a wasp. The female has a sting that is so painful and powerful that people have said "it could kill a cow." For this reason, the velvet ant's nickname is "cow killer." The velvet ant is covered in hair which can be red and black, completely white, silver or gold.

WEEVIL: The weevil is a type of beetle that is very small but has a very long, odd-shaped snout. This long snout is what gives the weevil its nickname of "snout beetle." Weevils can be destructive insects. The boll weevil is a type of weevil that attacks cotton crops by laying its eggs inside cotton bolls. When the eggs hatch, the young weevils eat their way out, destroying the cotton.

XYELIDAE: The Xyelidae are sawflies and are kinds of wasps. They can usually be found in conifers, which are trees and shrubs that bear cones. The Xyelidae are easy to spot because of the two large body parts sticking out from their heads. These appendages look more like legs than antennae. The Xyelidae fossils date back to the Triassic period of time, over 200 million years ago. This means that the Xyelidae existed with some types of dinosaurs!

YELLOW MEALWORM: The yellow mealworm is not a worm, but actually a type of beetle. The mealworm is often fed to pet reptiles and birds and can also be used as fishing bait. These insects can be purchased in most pet stores and through the Internet. If you buy several mealworms at a time, you should store them in a warm dry place, occasionally feeding them dry dog biscuits. If you have a strange appetite, you might even try eating the mealworm. Some people enjoy these insects when they are sautéed with vegetables, making them quite a tasty "mealworm!"

ZEBRA CATERPILLAR: The zebra caterpillar has two bright yellow stripes running along each side of the body that are separated by alternating black and white stripes running around the body. This insect is not considered a true pest, but can cause damage to some trees and flowers. The greatest damage from these insects occurs in summer months. In fact, they do not need to be told to eat their vegetables since they feed on cabbage, broccoli and cauliflower, leaving behind nothing but ragged-edged leaves.